Relationship Talk

Exploring Meaningful Questions Inspired by the Bahá'í Faith

Susanne M. Alexander and
Johanna Merritt Wu, PhD

Relationship Talk

ISBN: 978-1-940062-35-8 (Trade Paperback)
ISBN: 978-1-940062-36-5 (eBook)
Publisher: Marriage Transformation LLC
Printer: Ingram Spark; USA
https://www.marriagetransformation.com
susanne@marriagetransformation.com
+1-423-599-0153 (US Eastern)

©2024 by Marriage Transformation LLC, all international rights reserved. No part of this book may be electronically shared, scanned, uploaded, or reproduced by any means without the publisher's written permission. Violations are considered theft of the authors' and the publisher's intellectual property. Thank you for your respect for this legal copyright. Your adherence to this law grows positive spirit and respect throughout the world and brings us happiness.

If you wish to share the book, please direct people to an online bookstore or our website where they can purchase a copy. Brief excerpts may be quoted in study groups, newsletters, and media. The publisher welcomes inquiries about use.

This publication provides useful and educational information about couple relationships. If you need expert assistance, please meet with a competent professional counselor.

Cover Design: Steiner Graphics (with assistance from Neda Rahimi)
Cover Graphic: Tetiana Garkusha, iStock

Relationship Talk
What's Inside the Book

COME JOIN US
- **Intriguing Questions**
- **Why This Book?**
- **How to Use This Tool**
- **Including Spiritual Inspiration**

THE QUESTIONS BEGIN

1. Before You Meet Someone Special
2. Can You Be Friends Too?
3. Does Close or Far Matter?
4. What's in Your Character?
5. Are You Growing?
6. Is Character a Big Deal in Relationships?
7. Healing from Your Past
8. Checking Out the Family
9. What Do You Expect?
10. Using Your Creativity
11. What Works and What Doesn't
12. How Does the Spiritual Fit in?

13. What About Partnership?
14. Enjoying Being with a Partner
15. Having a Circle of Friends
16. Are You a Good Match?
17. What Are Your Priorities?
18. Talking and Listening to Each Other
19. Expressing Your Feelings
20. When Communication Gets Difficult
21. Consulting Through Challenges
22. Poor Communication Habits
23. Your Couple Interactions
24. Showing Appreciation and Love
25. Sex When You're Married
26. Sex When You're Single?
27. Being Faithful As a Goal
28. Becoming a Family
29. Parenting Together
30. All the Money Stuff
31. When Life Is Tough
32. Where Are You Going?
33. Are the Families Supportive?
34. Deciding to Marry
35. Do Your Parents Agree?
36. Creating Your Wedding
37. Being in Community Together

END PIECES
- **Sources of Quotations**
- **Meet Your Authors**
- **To Find Out More**

Come Join Us!

Relationship Talk

Intriguing Questions

When you hang out with friends or family, the topic of relationships is almost inevitable. How can you dive into the subject to better prepare yourself for the complexities of love and marriage?

Welcome to *Relationship Talk*!

Why This Book?

For 20 years, we've been writing wide-ranging and comprehensive books to help you create excellent relationships and build healthy marriages. You'll probably want to own these two listed below for further study as you explore the questions in *Relationship Talk*:

- *Starting with Me: Knowing Myself Before Finding a Partner*

- *Marriage Can Be Forever—Preparation Counts!: A Learning Guide Based on the Bahá'í Faith*

While sharing these tools, we've noticed a different need that's not being met. Often, friends or groups with a purpose want to take a deeper dive into discussing a relationship topic. We created this book to meet that need. Couples may also find the book useful.

How to Use This Tool

- You may toss the book around to each other and open to a page randomly; then ask or answer the question you find

- You could follow the questions page by page, in sequential order

Relationship Talk

- You could use this as a resource for starting a conversation or for prompting a deeper interaction

- You might consider how the topics and quotations in this book could be useful in future meaningful conversations with people you want to talk to more

- You can add in other game-like elements, such as those listed below:

    o   Draw your answer to a question, and have the others guess what you drew and what it meant

    o   Set a timer for how long someone has to come up with an answer

    o   Guess how others in the circle might respond to a given question

    o   Have everyone write down their answer, put them in a pile, and guess who said what

Relationship Talk

Including Spiritual Inspiration

Along with the questions, you'll see relevant excerpts of quotations from the Bahá'í Faith's teachings to offer insights that might inform your reflection or responses. The sources for the quotations are at the back of the book for reference. We anticipate people from diverse backgrounds and beliefs will use this book.

The Bahá'í teachings have enriched and transformed our lives and provide a foundation for all our life choices, so we're excited to share them with you. Some quotations were written in the 1800s and 1900s, and others were written more recently. While some were written in English initially, many were translated from Persian or Arabic, so there is variation in language usage. For example, when some words are translated as "man" in English, the original terms almost always imply "humanity" or "man" and "woman" interchangeably. Additionally, you may see words capitalized that you are used to seeing in lowercase

Relationship Talk

letters; this is often to demonstrate that something is significant or sacred.

As you engage in group discussions, you will likely have participants who love and worship God, others who aren't sure or are negative about anything spiritual, and everything in between. Some people find specific religious terms or concepts unappealing, perhaps due to negative associations or experiences. When we speak of God in the book, we mean the ultimate and infinite divine goodness that guides and loves all of humanity. If a term we use is uncomfortable, please use your preferred term.

Enjoy diving in and having intriguing conversations!

Note: If you wish to learn more about the Bahá'í Faith and better understand its teachings, a good source is https://www.bahai.org/.

Relationship Talk

The Questions Begin

Relationship Talk

1 - Before You Meet Someone Special

What do you think is the best age to get married? (if there is one)

What do you think are the signals that someone is mature enough and ready for a serious relationship?

What are your thoughts about preparing yourself for a relationship? Studying about marriage?

Relationship Talk

Should you have your whole life sorted out before having a serious relationship or getting married? OR
Is it okay to still be working on personal stuff? (Like showing responsibility, finishing your education, developing other lasting healthy friendships, accomplishing financial goals, and so on)

For reflection...

"... [Y]outh should [marry] while still young and in full possession of their physical vigor."

Relationship Talk

"There are advantages and disadvantages in whatever one does, and there is always some unpredictability about the future. An individual should decide on such matters in the light of his circumstances, possibilities and responsibilities. It may be best for you to consult with the members of your family and close friends who are familiar with your situation and whose wisdom and farsightedness you respect."

Relationship Talk

2 - Can You Be Friends Too?

How important are friendships to you? Do you expect your partner also to be a close friend?

Would having a partner affect some of your other important friendships? If so, how?

What do you think are the most foundational elements of a close friendship? Would you want those with a partner?

Relationship Talk

How could being close friends benefit a married couple?

For reflection...

"To the extent that the conversation continues beyond the initial encounter and veritable friendships are formed, an...effort...can become a catalyst for an enduring process of spiritual transformation."

"They are two helpmates, two intimate friends, who should be concerned about the welfare of each other."

3 - Does Close or Far Matter?

What could be the upsides of a long-distance relationship?

What might be difficult for you in a long-distance relationship?

How could you learn about a partner's character, background, family, and culture when you live near each other? What about when you live far away from each other?

Relationship Talk

For reflection...

"...[B]uilding a strong, united marriage requires persistence, effort, and the overcoming of many difficulties together. ... [Couples are advised] to get to know each other's characters thoroughly before taking this very important step. They must think not only of the effect on each other but of the effects of their characters on the children who will be the fruit of the marriage."

Relationship Talk

4 - What's in Your Character?

How do you think about or define "character"? And what are some essential facets of character to you?

Are virtues a part of a person's character? What are some examples?

What are some virtues you bring to a relationship?

Relationship Talk

For reflection...

"They must show forth such trustworthiness, such truthfulness and perseverance, such deeds and character that all mankind may profit by their example."

"... [T]he attributes of the people of faith are justice and fair-mindedness; forbearance and compassion and generosity; consideration for others; candor, trustworthiness, and loyalty; love and loving-kindness; devotion and determination and humanity."

5 - Are You Growing?

Do you reflect on your own mental, spiritual, and emotional well-being? Do you have a consistent way of doing that?

Do you think you have any blind spots where you don't see your strengths and areas for growth? How could you learn what these are?

Before getting into a relationship, what do you think people should work on personally for their health, well-being, and character development? Do you have approaches to foster your growth and development?

Are there parts of your character or virtues you hope to grow before being in a serious relationship?

For reflection...

"The most vital duty, in this day, is to purify your characters, to correct your manners, and improve your conduct."

"Every day, in the morning when arising you should compare today with

yesterday and see in what condition you are."

"Each of us is responsible for one life only, and that is our own. ... [T]he task of perfecting our own life and character is one that requires all our attention, our will-power and energy."

6 - Is Character a Big Deal in Relationships?

How could someone's character affect their relationships and their marriage?

What virtues of yours and others are most important to you?

Do you want your virtues to be similar to or different from those in a partner? How similar do you want your characters to be?

Relationship Talk

For reflection...

"A couple should study each other's character and spend time getting to know each other before they decide to marry...."

7 - Healing from Your Past

What are some ways to address and heal pain from past relationships?

If you currently have or did have a difficult family life, how do you think it might affect your future relationships?

What are your thoughts on how someone can heal from painful family experiences and have a healthy relationship or marriage?

For reflection...

"Illnesses which occur by reason of physical causes should be treated by doctors with medical remedies; those which are due to spiritual causes disappear through spiritual means...."

"Consultation is ... available for the individual in solving his own problems; he may consult with his Assembly, with his family and with his friends."

"Neither you nor your husband should hesitate to continue consulting professional marriage counselors, individually and together if possible, and also to take advantage of the supportive counseling which can come from wise and mature friends."

Relationship Talk

8 - Checking Out the Family

What important behaviors and lessons about relationships and marriage have you learned from your parents, grandparents, siblings, or others?

Are there examples of behaviors from relationships that you have seen in your extended family that you do not want to repeat?

What interactions would concern you if you observed them in your partner's family?

Relationship Talk

For reflection...

"Note ye how easily, where unity existeth in a given family, the affairs of that family are conducted; what progress the members of that family make, how they prosper in the world. Their concerns are in order, they enjoy comfort and tranquility, they are secure...."

"There should be a spirit of mutual respect and consideration between parents and children, in which the children turn to their parents for advice and direction, and the parents train and nurture their offspring. The fruit of this relationship is that the children grow into adulthood with their powers of discrimination and judgment refined, so that they can steer the course of their lives in a manner most conducive to their welfare."

Relationship Talk

9 - What Do You Expect?

What are some of your expectations about a relationship? Are they realistic and healthy? Do you have the same or different expectations of a marriage?

How can two people share their expectations of a relationship? How can this be done constructively and honestly?

Relationship Talk

How could each person strive to meet the other's reasonable expectations?

Could you have unrealistic expectations of a partner? Of a relationship? Of a marriage? What are some of them? How could you understand and address them?

For reflection...

"... [E]ach prospective marriage presents highly individualized relationships, and the decision to marry should preferably be made after acquaintanceship and exploration of

each other's character and background and, if necessary, with counsel from trusted friends."

"The Bahá'í teachings set clear prerequisites for marriage which, if carefully applied, minimize the possibility of a breakdown of this important institution. One such requirement is that the couple should independently choose each other and confidently have a mutual desire to be united in marriage, and such desire should be founded not only on love but also on mutual satisfaction arising from an investigation of the character of each other."

Relationship Talk

10 - Using Your Creativity

If your ideal relationship had a script, what genre would it be? (examples: a romantic comedy, drama, or maybe even a superhero flick?)

In your ideal relationship script, how would the characters interact? How would their healthy relationship develop and progress?

Are there song lyrics you think speak to a good relationship?

For reflection...

"...[A]ll the existing sciences and crafts, all the great undertakings and myriad discoveries of man were at one time hidden and concealed mysteries, and it is that all-encompassing human power that has discovered them and brought them forth from the invisible into the visible realm."

11 - What Works and What Doesn't

When it comes to a partner's behavior, what are your realistic and meaningful "must haves"? (Think about a wide array of mental, emotional, spiritual, or physical behaviors)

What partner behaviors or past experiences would be "deal-breakers" in your relationship? (Think about a wide array of mental, emotional, spiritual, or physical behaviors)

Relationship Talk

When you think about what might make a relationship healthy and happy for you, what are some positive "green flags" and behaviors?

What would be some "red flags" of potential trouble ahead for a relationship?

For reflection...

"As to qualities a man should look for in seeking a life partner, no universal guidelines can be set forth as whatever characteristics or conditions one considers essential are, of course, subjective and relative...."

Relationship Talk

"... [T]hey must establish between them a level of openness and close communication. They will themselves determine if, when and how they will share past and personal experiences."

12 - How Does the Spiritual Fit in?

For you, how might spirituality or religion contribute to the quality of a serious relationship? Of a marriage?

What aspects of spirituality and religion would be important to you to practice together in a relationship? (examples: prayer, study, gatherings, community involvement, service activities with others...)

What words or actions could show that you have a spiritual connection in your relationship or marriage?

For reflection...

"... [H]usband and wife should be united both physically and spiritually, that they may ever improve the spiritual life of each other, and may enjoy everlasting unity."

"...[A]bide with each other in the closest companionship, and to be even as a single soul."

"...[A]ssess your overall purpose in life and use that assessment as the framework upon which to make your decision."

13 - What About Partnership?

What does equality in a relationship and treating each other equally mean and look like to you?

What actions demonstrate equality related to communication, housework, professional lives, child-rearing...?

What are the messages from your culture about the equality of women and men? What are your beliefs?

For reflection...

"The world of humanity has two wings—one is women and the other men. Not until both wings are equally developed can the bird fly."

"There is a right hand and a left hand in the human body, functionally equal in service and administration. If either proves defective, the defect will naturally extend to the other by involving the completeness of the whole...."

Relationship Talk

14 – Enjoying Being with a Partner

What activities would be fun and enjoyable for you to do with a partner?

Is it important to you to share a sense of humor with a partner? How do you get a partner to laugh?

What would be signs that you and your partner are comfortable and relaxed together?

Relationship Talk

What would show that you manage stress well together?

What are some effective ways to handle if you become unhappy, frustrated with, or stressed by your partner?

For reflection...

"... [T]rue happiness and joy and humor that are parts of a balanced life that includes serious thought, compassion and humble servitude to God are characteristics that enrich life and add to its radiance."

Relationship Talk

"... [L]aughter should not ... be indulged in at the expense of the feelings of others."

Relationship Talk

15 - Having a Circle of Friends

What do you see could be a positive balance of having friends other than just your partner? What activities would you do with them, separately and together?

If the two of you decided it would be healthy to expand your circle of friends, how would you do that?

What could be the benefits and challenges of having friends who are couples?

Relationship Talk

For reflection...

"Be worthy of the trust of thy neighbor, and look upon him with a bright and friendly face."

"One must see in every human being only that which is worthy of praise. When this is done, one can be a friend to the whole human race. If, however, we look at people from the standpoint of their faults, then being a friend to them is a formidable task."

"Do not be content with showing friendship in words alone, let your heart burn with loving kindness for all who may cross your path."

Relationship Talk

16 - Are You a Good Match?

As a couple, what signs would show that you are generally in unity and harmony with one another?

What are some ways to create unity and harmony, even when two people are quite different?

How could a couple check in with each other regularly about the health of their relationship?

Relationship Talk

What words and actions could draw you closer together if you feel distant from your partner?

For you, what are some compatible personality traits in a partner? What are some personality differences that you might find difficult to live with?

For reflection...

"... Bahá'u'lláh has stated that the purpose of marriage is to promote unity...."

"In the context of the society in which your family now lives, a society in which materialism, self-centeredness and

failing marriages are all too common, your sons may well feel that it is wise to have a long period of courtship in which the prospective partners spend much time together and become thoroughly acquainted with each other's character, background and family."

Relationship Talk

17 - What Are Your Priorities?

What are your priorities in your life? Would you see these staying the same or changing with marriage?

What are signs a partner has made your relationship a priority? What might indicate that it's not a priority?

Are there ways a partner may spend their time that would be difficult for you to accept?

Relationship Talk

For reflection...

"Blessed and happy is he that ariseth to promote the best interests of the peoples and kindreds of the earth."

"Under ordinary circumstances, [everyone has] to make many choices in life between what they consider their duty and what might lead to a more ideal personal state for them. Prayerfully, wisely and conscientiously, individuals must settle these matters for themselves."

"... [T]he unity of your family should take priority over any other consideration."

Relationship Talk

18 - Talking and Listening to Each Other

How does good communication—both speaking and listening—contribute to a healthy relationship?

What communication skills do individuals need to interact and cooperate constructively as a couple?

What communication skills are you good at using consistently?

Relationship Talk

What communication, consultation, and conflict management patterns do you want to establish in your current or future partnership?

How important is it to you to have a truthful partner? What would your response be to discovering that they lie?

For reflection...

"... [T]he tongue is for mentioning what is good...."

"Truthfulness is the foundation of all human virtues...."

"... [R]emember that at the very root of the [Bahá'í Faith] lies the principle of the undoubted right of the individual to self-expression, his freedom to declare his conscience and set forth his views. ...Let us also bear in mind that the keynote of the Cause of God is not dictatorial authority but humble fellowship, not arbitrary power, but the spirit of frank and loving consultation. Nothing short of the spirit of a true Bahá'í can hope to reconcile the principles of mercy and justice, of freedom and submission, of the sanctity of the right of the individual and of self-surrender, of vigilance, discretion and prudence on the one hand, and fellowship, candor, and courage on the other."

"Also relevant to what is said, and how, is when it is said. For speech, as for so many other things, there is a season."

Relationship Talk

19 - Expressing Your Feelings

What helps you identify what you are feeling? What are some ways you express those feelings?

What expressions of feelings seem to be from your heart and are constructive in a relationship? Which expressions seem destructive instead?

What negative emotions might a partner express that are difficult for you to deal with? How could you and your partner express unpleasant feelings honestly and without causing injury?

For reflection...

"The human heart resembleth a mirror. When this is purified, human hearts are attuned and reflect one another, and thus spiritual emotions are generated."

"... [T]he function of language is to portray the mysteries and secrets of human hearts. The heart is like a box, and language is the key. Only by using the key can we open the box and observe the gems it contains."

Relationship Talk

20 - When Communication Gets Difficult

What do you think causes couples to fight rather than connect and communicate effectively?

What are some ways that you and a partner could prevent conflict between you?

Are there opinions or perspectives you would have trouble accepting in a partner because they would consistently cause difficulties between you?

Relationship Talk

How could you best handle conflict between you and a partner?

For reflection...

"... [L]et not every insignificant matter become the cause of disagreement."

"When you notice that a stage has been reached when enmity and threats are about to occur, you should immediately postpone discussion of the subject, until wranglings, disputations, and loud talk vanish, and a propitious time is at hand."

"They must in every matter search out the truth and not insist upon their own opinion, for stubbornness and persistence in one's views will lead

ultimately to discord and wrangling and the truth will remain hidden."

"...[T]he term 'conflict' encompasses a variety of conditions, ranging from contention to friendly disagreement. ... Bahá'u'lláh has forbidden His followers to engage in contention. He has also stressed the importance of consultation. Indeed, consultation within the family, employing full and frank discussion and animated by awareness of the need for moderation and balance, can be the panacea for domestic conflict."

21 - Consulting Through Challenges

What do you think contributes to building comfort and the freedom to share thoughts and feelings between partners?

What are your thoughts about individuals in a couple making decisions with or without consulting together?

What specific behaviors could assist couples to reach decisions in unity?

What virtues could you apply together with being frank and honest, so your words would be easier for your partner to hear?

Would you communicate differently if the topic may be conflictual? (examples: politics, spending patterns, different beliefs...)

For reflection...

"In all things it is necessary to consult...inasmuch as it is and will always be a cause of awareness and of awakening and a source of good and well-being."

Relationship Talk

"...[C]onsultation must have for its object the investigation of truth. He who expresses an opinion should not voice it as correct and right but set it forth as a contribution to the consensus of opinion, for the light of reality becomes apparent when two opinions coincide."

"There can...be no majority where only two parties are involved, as in the case of a husband and wife. There are, therefore, times when a wife should defer to her husband, and times when a husband should defer to his wife, but neither should ever unjustly dominate the other."

"Consultation is no easy skill to learn, requiring as it does the subjugation of all egotism and unruly passions, the cultivation of frankness and freedom of thought as well as courtesy, openness

Relationship Talk

of mind and wholehearted acquiescence in a majority decision."

Relationship Talk

22 - Poor Communication Habits

How do you approach difficult conversations with someone? Are you usually able to do it without triggering their defensiveness?

When someone shares something difficult with you, do you tend to react defensively or listen fully? What might help you listen better and use what they shared for self-improvement?

What do you think of backbiting and gossip? Is it common among you and your friends? What could be some strategies for preventing it?

For reflection...

"... [T]he tongue is a smoldering fire, and excess of speech a deadly poison. ... [B]ackbiting quencheth the light of the heart, and extinguisheth the life of the soul."

"... [M]an can receive no greater gift than this, that he rejoice another's heart."

"Content, volume, style, tact, wisdom, timeliness are among the critical factors in determining the effects of speech for good or evil."

Relationship Talk

"There is a distinction to be made between speaking about the mistakes and shortcomings of others, which is backbiting, and protecting someone from the harmful or evil intentions of an abuser, a chronic liar or a sociopath."

Relationship Talk

23 - Your Couple Interactions

How can you show care and thoughtfulness for your partner's needs and preferences—even when it's inconvenient for you?

How could you make your partner's life easier and more pleasant?

What words and actions would show that your partner cares and is thoughtful of your needs and preferences?

Relationship Talk

For reflection...

"A kindly tongue is the lodestone of the hearts of men. It is the bread of the spirit, it clotheth the words with meaning, it is the fountain of the light of wisdom and understanding...."

"I admonish you to observe courtesy, for above all else it is the prince of virtues."

"... [W]ed Thou in the heaven of Thy mercy these two birds of the nest of Thy love, and make them the means of attracting perpetual grace; that from the union of these two seas of love a wave of tenderness may surge and cast the pearls of pure and goodly issue on the shore of life."

Relationship Talk

24 - Showing Appreciation and Love

What are some ways you like to show appreciation to someone close to you?

How can your partner best show they appreciate you and what you do?

What do you think are some essential ways to show love in a relationship or marriage?

Relationship Talk

What are the most important ways a partner shows they love you?

For reflection...

"The love between husband and wife must not be purely physical, nay, rather, it must be spiritual and heavenly. These two souls should be considered as one soul. How difficult it would be to divide a single soul!"

"We can never exert the influence over others which we can exert over ourselves. If we are better, if we show love, patience, and understanding of the weakness of others, if we seek to never criticize but rather encourage, others will do likewise…."

Relationship Talk

25 - Sex When You're Married

What do you think could increase a married couple feeling comfortable talking about sex?

How would you describe a healthy sexual relationship within marriage?

How might it affect your relationship or marriage if one or both of you are uncertain about your gender identity or are in the process of changing it?

For reflection...

"The world today is submerged, amongst other things, in an over-exaggeration of the importance of physical love, and a dearth of spiritual values. In as far as possible the believers should try to realize this and rise above the level of their fellow-men who are, typical of all decadent periods in history, placing so much over-emphasis on the purely physical side of mating. Outside of their normal, legitimate married life they should seek to establish bonds of comradeship and love which are eternal and founded on the spiritual life of man, not on his physical life. This is one of the many fields in which it is incumbent on the Bahá'ís to set the example and lead the way to a true human standard of life, when the soul of man is exalted and his body but the tool for his enlightened

spirit. Needless to say this does not preclude the living of a perfectly normal sex life in its legitimate channel of marriage."

"...[T]he Bahá'í Faith recognizes the value of the sex impulse and holds that the institution of marriage has been established as the channel of its rightful expression."

Relationship Talk

26 - Sex When You're Single?

What is your understanding of chastity and how it connects to personal well-being?

How do you think chastity, including not being physically intimate before marriage, affects the health of a relationship and marriage?

If you and your partner choose not to be physically intimate before marriage, what could support you in maintaining that commitment to wait until after the wedding?

What are the possible adverse effects of having sex in an unmarried relationship?

For reflection...

"Such a chaste and holy life, with its implications of modesty, purity, temperance, decency, and clean-mindedness, involves no less than the exercise of moderation in all that pertains to dress, language, amusements, and all artistic and literary avocations. It demands daily vigilance in the control of one's carnal desires and corrupt inclinations. ...

Relationship Talk

"It must be remembered, however, that the maintenance of such a high standard of moral conduct is not to be associated or confused with any form of asceticism, or of excessive and bigoted puritanism. The standard inculcated by Bahá'u'lláh seeks, under no circumstances, to deny anyone the legitimate right and privilege to derive the fullest advantage and benefit from the manifold joys, beauties, and pleasures with which the world has been so plentifully enriched by an All-Loving Creator."

"Chastity in no way implies withdrawal from human relationships. It liberates people from the tyranny of the ubiquity of sex. A person who is in control of his sexual impulses is enabled to have profound and enduring friendships with many people, both men and women, without ever sullying that unique and

Relationship Talk

priceless bond that should unite [husband] and wife."

27 - Being Faithful As a Goal

What are your thoughts about limiting contact or friendships with previous partners or those you have felt attracted to? What could be healthy or unhealthy about that approach?

Do you tend to be trusting or wary about a partner's faithfulness?

How could having a solid friendship between you and a

Relationship Talk

partner help when you feel less attracted?

How could your relationship be affected if one of you feels strongly attracted to someone else? How would you address it?

What could be the implications for personal and relationship well-being if either or both of you use pornography?

For reflection...

"Chastity implies both before and after marriage an unsullied, chaste sex life.

Relationship Talk

Before marriage absolutely chaste, after marriage absolutely faithful to one's chosen companion. Faithful in all sexual acts, faithful in word and in deed."

Relationship Talk

28 - Becoming a Family

When envisioning the dynamics of a family you are building with a partner, what behaviors do you imagine would foster a sense of happiness and unity?

What might indicate to you that someone would be an excellent partner to raise children with?

If you already have one or more children, what are your thoughts about introducing them to a potential partner?

Relationship Talk

If you have children now, what could a partner do to communicate to your children that they are valued?

For reflection...

"It is highly important for man to raise a family. So long as he is young, because of youthful self-complacency, he does not realize its significance, but this will be a source of regret when he grows old...."

Relationship Talk

29 - Parenting Together

What do you think might be or is a wonderful part of being a parent?

What are your fears about being a parent, if any?

How would you approach the development of your children? (examples: moral character, spiritual, mental, emotional, physical...)

What are your philosophies about discipline for children? How could you learn more about this topic?

How would you respond if your partner has different views on disciplining children?

For reflection...

"The training which a child first receives through his mother constitutes the strongest foundation for his future development...."

"Independent of the level of their education, parents are in a critical position to shape the spiritual development of their children. They

should not ever underestimate their capacity to mold their children's moral character."

Relationship Talk

30 - All the Money Stuff

What are your attitudes and approaches to work? What attitudes and approaches do you want in a partner?

What financial management topics are essential for you and a partner to agree on before marriage for the best cooperation?

What could financial responsibility look like in a

healthy marriage? What about financial generosity?

How could you better understand each of your approaches to handling money?

For reflection...

"It is incumbent upon each one of you to engage in some occupation—such as a craft, a trade or the like. We have exalted your engagement in such work to the rank of worship of the one true God."

"The acquisition of wealth is a case in point; it is acceptable and praiseworthy to the extent that it serves as a means

for achieving higher ends—for meeting one's basic necessities, for fostering the progress of one's family, for promoting the welfare of society, and for contributing to the establishment of a world civilization. But to make the accumulation of wealth the central purpose of one's life is unworthy of any human being."

"... [T]he circumstances of the partners vary from case to case and much depends on their attitudes towards material comforts. Many couples are able to be extremely happy with relatively little income."

Relationship Talk

31 - When Life Is Tough

What do you see as the purpose and value of going through difficulties?

When going through tough times, either between partners or from external factors, what do you think are the essential virtues and best coping skills to address issues?

What would you want to know about how a partner responded

to or solved past problems? About their resiliency?

If you or your partner have health challenges, what do you think are the ideal ways to support one another? What resources can you draw on beyond just the two of you? (examples: physical, mental, emotional, spiritual...)

For reflection...

"... [S]uffering, although an inescapable reality, can nevertheless be utilized as a means for the attainment of happiness. ... Suffering is both a reminder and a guide. It stimulates us to better adapt

ourselves to our environmental conditions, and thus leads the way to self-improvement."

"When two believers begin to investigate each other's character with the possibility of marriage in mind, they must establish between them a level of openness and close communication. They will themselves determine if, when and how they will share past and personal experiences. In this process, it is necessary to reconcile a variety of spiritual principles and obligations. Truthfulness and trustworthiness are essential of course, yet other aspects of the teachings must be weighed, such as Shoghi Effendi's guidance that while a believer may choose to acknowledge to another a wrong or fault of character, one is not obliged to do so."

Relationship Talk

32 - Where Are You Going?

When you reflect on what you want your marriage to be like, what do you see as its most essential features?

What are the benefits of having a shared vision for your relationship or future marriage? What might be some important elements of that vision?

What goals could ground your shared vision in practical actions?

For reflection...

"... [U]nity and love should increase day by day between husband and wife, so that they become one soul, one spirit and one body."

"... [T]he life of a married couple should resemble the life of the angels in heaven—a life full of joy and spiritual delight, a life of unity and concord, a friendship both mental and physical. The home should be orderly and well-organized. Their ideas and thoughts should be like the rays of the sun of truth and the radiance of the brilliant stars in the heavens. ... They should ... manifest true and sincere love towards each other...."

33 - Are the Families Supportive?

Is it important to you to build relationships with each other's families as you get to know each other? If so, what do you see as the benefits?

What's your ideal level of family involvement and support? Would it be different for you if it's your family compared to your partner's family?

What potential benefits could an extended family realize from a healthy marriage between you and your partner?

For reflection...

"If thou wouldst show kindness and consideration to thy parents so that they may feel generally pleased, this would also please Me, for parents must be highly respected and it is essential that they feel contented...."

"... [A] fundamental unity is that of the family."

"... [M]arriage can be a source of well-being, conveying a sense of security and spiritual happiness. However, it is not something that just happens. For marriage to become a haven of contentment it requires the cooperation

*of the marriage partners themselves,
and the assistance of their families…."*

Relationship Talk

34 - Deciding to Marry

What are the essential steps that you and your partner should take before deciding to get married?

What would indicate that it's wise for you to consult with others before deciding to marry, either individually or together with a partner?

What level of involvement do you want your parents to have as you contemplate marriage? What are the upsides and downsides of consulting them?

What significance do you place on you and your partner independently choosing to marry, free from external pressure or interference?

For reflection...

"... [T]he couple should independently choose each other and confidently have a mutual desire to be united in marriage, and such desire should be founded not only on love but also on mutual satisfaction arising from an investigation of the character of each other."

Relationship Talk

"... [P]arents do not have the right to interfere in their children's actual choice of a prospective partner...."

Relationship Talk

35 - Do Your Parents Agree?

What are your thoughts on seeking approval or consent from your parents to get married?

What could be positive outcomes from receiving consent from your parents for your marriage?

How do you think you would respond if one or more parents refused to give consent for you to marry?

For reflection...

"... [M]arriage is dependent upon the consent of both parties. Desiring to establish love, unity and harmony amidst Our servants, We have conditioned it, once the couple's wish is known, upon the permission of their parents, lest enmity and rancor should arise amongst them."

"Bahá'u'lláh has clearly stated the consent of all living parents is required for a Bahá'í marriage. This applies whether the parents are Bahá'ís or non-Bahá'ís, divorced for years or not. This great law He has laid down to strengthen the social fabric, to knit closer the ties of the home, to place a certain gratitude and respect in the hearts of children for those who have given them life and sent their souls out

on the eternal journey towards their Creator."

Relationship Talk

36 - Creating Your Wedding

When you reflect on what you might want your wedding to look like, what do you see as its most important features?

What could contribute to the wedding's simplicity and beauty if that's important to you?

What might you incorporate into your wedding ceremony to express your commitment to each other and your marriage?

Relationship Talk

What might you incorporate in your wedding to promote and build family unity?

For reflection...

"It is my fervent hope that...this marriage may bring about joy and radiance, and may gladden and cheer the friends—and that through it, a Bahá'í family may shine forth...the descendants of which will become manifestations of divine grace and bounty in the ages and centuries to come."

"... [T]his ceremony should be as simple as possible...."

Relationship Talk

37 - Being in Community Together

Do you value active religious community participation for yourself, for you and your partner, and for your future family? (examples: devotional or worship gatherings, study or learning activities, children's classes, junior youth activities...)

Do you tend to be hopeful or feel despair about the state of the world? What potential advantages could there be for you and a partner of being involved in activities to address issues?

If you and your partner decide to contribute your time and resources to improve your neighborhood or the wider civic or world community, what activities or services would you find appealing and valuable?

What are your preferences for who is involved in religious or community-betterment activities? (examples: as individuals, together as partners, the whole family, a mix...)

Relationship Talk

For reflection...

"Blessed and happy is he that ariseth to promote the best interests of the peoples and kindreds of the earth."

"And if we widen out the sphere of unity a little [from a family] to include the inhabitants of a village who seek to be loving and united, who associate with and are kind to one another, what great advances they will be seen to make, how secure and protected they will be. Then let us widen out the sphere a little more, let us take the inhabitants of a city, all of them together: if they establish the strongest bonds of unity among themselves, how far they will progress, even in a brief period and what power they will exert. And if the sphere of unity be still further widened out, that is, if the inhabitants of a whole country develop peaceable

hearts, and if with all their hearts and souls they yearn to cooperate with one another and to live in unity, and if they become kind and loving to one another, that country will achieve undying joy and lasting glory. Peace will it have, and plenty, and vast wealth."

"The true basis of [family] unity is service...."

"They are committed to the prosperity of all, recognizing that the welfare of individuals rests in the welfare of society at large. They are loyal citizens who eschew partisanship and the contest for worldly power. Instead, they are focused on transcending differences, harmonizing perspectives, and promoting the use of consultation for making decisions. They emphasize qualities and attitudes—such as trustworthiness, cooperation, and

forbearance—that are building blocks of a stable social order. They champion rationality and science as essential for human progress. They advocate tolerance and understanding, and with the inherent oneness of humanity uppermost in their minds, they view everyone as a potential partner to collaborate with, and they strive to foster fellow feeling even among groups who may traditionally have been hostile to one another. They are conscious of how the forces of materialism are at work around them, and their eyes are wide open to the many injustices that persist in the world, yet they are equally clear sighted about the creative power of unity and humanity's capacity for altruism."

Relationship Talk

End

Pieces

Relationship Talk

Sources of Quotations

1. **Before You Meet Someone Special**
- On behalf of the Universal House of Justice, "Investigation of Character, Courtship Practices, and Selection of a Marriage Partner", #5
- On behalf of the Universal House of Justice, "Choosing a Profession", #13

2. **Can You Be Friends Too?**
- Universal House of Justice, *Framework for Action*, #14.4
- 'Abdu'l-Bahá, *Selections from the Writings of 'Abdu'l-Bahá*, #92

3. **Does Close or Far Matter?**
- On behalf of the Universal House of Justice, "Investigation of Character, Courtship Practices, and Selection of a Marriage Partner", #11

4. **What's in Your Character?**
- Bahá'u'lláh, quoted in Shoghi Effendi, *Advent of Divine Justice*, p. 23

Relationship Talk

- 'Abdu'l-Bahá, *Secret of Divine Civilization*, pp. 55-56

5. **Are You Growing?**
- 'Abdu'l-Bahá, *Selections from the Writings of 'Abdu'l-Bahá*, #2
- 'Abdu'l-Bahá, *Lights of Guidance*, #1485
- On behalf of Shoghi Effendi, *Compilations of Compilations, Vol. II*, #1272

6. **Is Character a Big Deal in Relationships?**
- On behalf of the Universal House of Justice, *Lights of Guidance*, #1269

7. **Healing from Your Past**
- 'Abdu'l-Bahá, *Selections from the Writings of 'Abdu'l-Bahá*, #133
- On behalf of the Universal House of Justice to an individual, November 29, 1982; "Understanding Tests" memorandum from the Research Department of the Universal House of Justice, July 17, 1989
- On behalf of the Universal House of Justice, "To Set the World in Order: Building and Preserving Strong Marriages", a compilation prepared by the Research

Relationship Talk

Department of the Universal House of Justice, August 2023, #67

8. **Checking Out the Family**
- 'Abdu'l-Bahá, *Selections from the Writings of 'Abdu'l-Bahá*, #221
- On behalf of the Universal House of Justice, July 25, 1988, quoted in John F. Skeaff, *Consent of Parents* (out of print), p. 27

9. **What Do You Expect?**
- On behalf of the Universal House of Justice, "Investigation of Character, Courtship Practices, and Selection of a Marriage Partner", #9
- On behalf of the Universal House of Justice, "Investigation of Character, Courtship Practices, and Selection of a Marriage Partner", #18

10. **Using Your Creativity**
- 'Abdu'l-Bahá, *Some Answered Questions*, #48

Relationship Talk

11. **What Works and What Doesn't**
- On behalf of the Universal House of Justice, "Investigation of Character, Courtship Practices, and Selection of a Marriage Partner", #13
- On behalf of the Universal House of Justice, "Investigation of Character, Courtship Practices, and Selection of a Marriage Partner", #20

12. **How Does the Spiritual Fit in?**
- 'Abdu'l-Bahá, *Selections from the Writings of 'Abdu'l-Bahá*, #86
- 'Abdu'l-Bahá, *Selections from the Writings of 'Abdu'l-Bahá*, #92
- On behalf of the Universal House of Justice, "Bahá'í Marriage, Selected Extracts from the Bahá'í Writings and Communications by and on behalf of the Universal House of Justice, National Spiritual Assembly Resource Material"; Bahá'í World Centre; August 2022; #24

13. **What About Partnership?**
- 'Abdu'l-Bahá, *Selections from the Writings of 'Abdu'l-Bahá*, #227

- 'Abdu'l-Bahá, *Promulgation of Universal Peace*, #51

14. **Enjoying Being with a Partner**
- Shoghi Effendi; On behalf of the Universal House of Justice, *Compilations of Compilations, Vol. I*, #138
- On behalf of the Universal House of Justice; quoted in Research Department of the Universal House of Justice Memorandum, "The 'Humorist'", January 12, 1997

15. **Having a Circle of Friends**
- Bahá'u'lláh, *Gleanings from the Writings of Bahá'u'lláh*, #CXXX
- 'Abdu'l-Bahá, *Selections of the Writings of 'Abdu'l-Bahá*, #144
- 'Abdu'l-Bahá, *Paris Talks*, #1

16. **Are You a Good Match?**
- On behalf of Shoghi Effendi, *Compilation of Compilations, Vol. I*, #910
- On behalf of the Universal House of Justice, "Investigation of Character, Courtship

Relationship Talk

Practices, and Selection of a Marriage Partner", #17

17. What Are Your Priorities?
- Bahá'u'lláh, *Gleanings from the Writings of Bahá'u'lláh*, #CXVII
- On behalf of Shoghi Effendi, *Uncompiled Published Letters*, April 5, 1951, to the National Spiritual Assembly of Central America
- On behalf of the Universal House of Justice, "To Set the World in Order: Building and Preserving Strong Marriages", a compilation prepared by the Research Department of the Universal House of Justice, August 2023, #63

18. Talking and Listening to Each Other
- Bahá'u'lláh, *Tablets of Bahá'u'lláh*, #15
- 'Abdu'l-Bahá, quoted in Shoghi Effendi, *Advent of Divine Justice*, p. 26
- Shoghi Effendi, *Bahá'í Administration*, pp. 63-64
- Universal House of Justice, December 29, 1988, "Individual Rights and Freedoms", pp. 12-13

Relationship Talk

19. **Expressing Your Feelings**
- 'Abdu'l-Bahá, *Selections from the Writings of 'Abdu'l-Bahá*, #70
- 'Abdu'l-Bahá, *Promulgation of Universal Peace*, #12

20. **When Communication Gets Difficult**
- 'Abdu'l-Bahá, quoted in Shoghi Effendi *Principles of Bahá'í Administration*, p. 48
- 'Abdu'l-Bahá, *Lights of Guidance*, #587
- Shoghi Effendi, *Bahá'í Administration*, p. 22
- On behalf of the Universal House of Justice to an individual, September 24, 2014

21. **Consulting Through Challenges**
- Bahá'u'lláh, *Compilation of Compilations, Vol. I*, #170
- 'Abdu'l-Bahá, *Promulgation of Universal Peace*, #31
- Shoghi Effendi, *Lights of Guidance*, #751
- Universal House of Justice, *Messages from the Universal House of Justice, 1963 to 1986*, p. 95

Relationship Talk

22. **Poor Communication Habits**
- Bahá'u'lláh, *Gleanings from the Writings of Bahá'u'lláh*, #CXXV
- 'Abdu'l-Bahá, *Selections from the Writings of 'Abdu'l-Bahá*, #174
- Universal House of Justice, "Individual Rights and Freedoms", p. 16
- On behalf of the Universal House of Justice, "Investigation of Character, Courtship Practices, and Selection of a Marriage Partner", #20

23. **Your Couple Interactions**
- Bahá'u'lláh, *Gleanings from the Writings of Bahá'u'lláh*, #CXXXII
- Bahá'u'lláh, *Tablets of Bahá'u'lláh*, #7
- 'Abdu'l-Bahá, *Bahá'í Prayers* (US 2002), pp. 119-120

24. **Showing Appreciation and Love**
- 'Abdu'l-Bahá, *Compilation of Compilations, Vol. II*, #2308
- On behalf of Shoghi Effendi, *Lights of Guidance*, #291

Relationship Talk

25. **Sex When You're Married**
- On behalf of Shoghi Effendi, quoted in *Messages from the Universal House of Justice, 1968-1973*, pp. 108-109
- On behalf of the Universal House of Justice to an individual believer, April 17, 2017

26. **Sex When You're Single?**
- Shoghi Effendi, *Advent of Divine Justice*, pp. 25, 28
- On behalf of the Universal House of Justice, *Compilation of Compilations, Vol. I*, #128

27. **Being Faithful As a Goal**
- On behalf of Shoghi Effendi, quoted in *Messages from the Universal House of Justice, 1968-1973*, p. 108

28. **Becoming a Family**
- 'Abdu'l-Bahá, *Lights of Guidance*, #733

29. **Parenting Together**
- On behalf of Shoghi Effendi, *Compilation of Compilations, Vol. I,* #674
- Universal House of Justice, "To Set the World in Order: Building and Preserving

Strong Marriages", compiled by the Research Department of the Universal House of Justice, August 2023, #28

30. **All the Money Stuff**
- Bahá'u'lláh, *Kitáb-i-Aqdas*, #K33
- Universal House of Justice to the Bahá'ís of Iran, April 2, 2010
- On behalf of the Universal House of Justice, "Investigation of Character, Courtship Practices, and Selection of a Marriage Partner", #13

31. **When Life Is Tough**
- On behalf of Shoghi Effendi, May 29, 1935, unpublished; "Understanding Tests" memorandum from the Research Department of the Universal House of Justice, July 17, 1989
- On behalf of the Universal House of Justice, "Investigation of Character, Courtship Practices, and Selection of a Marriage Partner", #20

32. Where Are You Going?
- 'Abdu'l-Bahá, "To Set the World in Order: Building and Preserving Strong Marriages", compiled by the Research Department of the Universal House of Justice, August 2023, #8
- 'Abdu'l-Bahá, *Lights of Guidance*, #860

33. Are the Families Supportive?
- 'Abdu'l-Bahá, *Compilation of Compilations, Vol. I*, #843
- Universal House of Justice, *Lights of Guidance*, #734
- On behalf of the Universal House of Justice, *Compilation of Compilations, Vol. II*, #2161

34. Deciding to Marry
- On behalf of the Universal House of Justice, "Investigation of Character, Courtship Practices, and Selection of a Marriage Partner", #18
- On behalf of the Universal House of Justice, "Investigation of Character, Courtship Practices, and Selection of a Marriage Partner", #17

Relationship Talk

35. **Do Your Parents Agree?**
- Bahá'u'lláh, *Kitáb-i-Aqdas*, #K65
- On behalf of Shoghi Effendi, "To Set the World in Order: Building and Preserving Strong Marriages", compiled by the Research Department of the Universal House of Justice, August 2023, #54

36. **Creating Your Wedding**
- 'Abdu'l-Bahá, "To Set the World in Order: Building and Preserving Strong Marriages", compiled by the Research Department of the Universal House of Justice, August 2023, #18
- On behalf of Shoghi Effendi, *Lights of Guidance*, #1298

37. **Being in Community Together**
- Bahá'u'lláh, *Gleanings from the Writings of Bahá'u'lláh*, #CXVII
- 'Abdu'l-Bahá, *Selections from the Writings of 'Abdu'l-Bahá*, #221
- On behalf of Shoghi Effendi, *Compilation of Compilations, Vol. II*, #2334

Relationship Talk

- Universal House of Justice, to the Conference of the Continental Boards of Counsellors, December 30, 2021

Relationship Talk

Meet Your Authors

Susanne M. Alexander is a Relationship and Marriage Educator, Certified Pre-Marriage and Marriage Coach, and certified character specialist with her company, Marriage Transformation®. She is passionate about accompanying individuals and couples to make good relationship and marriage choices through knowledge and skill-building.
https://marriagetransformation.com

Johanna Merritt Wu, PhD, is an organizational psychologist who specializes in executive coaching, leadership development, corporate mergers, and teamwork. She leads workshops for businesses and on marriage preparation. She hosts several weekly devotionals and study circles and has led a weekly youth group since 2008.
https://www.johannawu.com/

Relationship Talk

To Find Out More

Suppose you want to dive deeper into preparing yourself as an individual for a relationship or as a couple for marriage. In that case, we encourage you to buy and use these books from your favorite bookstore:

- *Starting with Me: Knowing Myself Before Finding a Partner* (3rd ed.)
- *Marriage Can Be Forever—Preparation Counts!* (4th ed.)

You can participate in online courses at:
https://www.transformationlearningcenter.com/
And, find other resources and services at:
https://marriagetransformation.com/
https://bahaimarriage.net/

Marriage Transformation® dynamically empowers individuals and couples to engage in skillful, character-based communications and actions that contribute to excellent relationships and happy, unified marriages and families that serve others.

www.ingramcontent.com/pod-product-compliance
Lightning Source LLC
Chambersburg PA
CBHW070113080526
44586CB00013B/1279